PRAYING THE BIBLE

for Your

BABY

PRAYING THE BIBLE

for Your

BABY

HEATHER HARPHAM KOPP

WATERBROOK
PRESS

COLORADO SPRINGS

PRAYING THE BIBLE FOR YOUR BABY
PUBLISHED BY WATERBROOK PRESS
5446 North Academy Boulevard, Suite 200, Colorado Springs, Colorado 80918
A division of Bantam Doubleday Dell Publishing Group, Inc.

Scriptures in this book, unless otherwise noted, are from
The Holy Bible, New International Version
© 1973, 1978, 1984 by International Bible Society,
used by permission of Zondervan Publishing House
Also cited, *The Living Bible* (TLB)
© 1971 by Tyndale House Publishers

ISBN 1-57856-086-1

From birth I was cast upon you;
from my mother's womb you have been my God.

PSALM 22:10

Contents

Section Four

MY NAME IS MOMMY

Section Five

I ONLY BLINKED

Acknowledgments

Special thanks to Nancy Kennedy and Erin Healy, gifted writers and moms who shared in the "pregnancy" of this book and who contributed greatly to this collection of prayers. I appreciate you so much!

Thanks also to my sister, Katherine Hillis Mosby, who provided editorial assistance and constant inspiration as her belly grew larger by the day with Baby Addison.

Once again, I am grateful to my editors at WaterBrook Press, Traci Mullins and Carol Bartley, for their excellent input and painstaking attention to detail.

Praying from Day One

Ask any woman who's given birth to a baby what it was like, and she'll probably reply, "Oh, it was so terrible! I've never been in so much pain…" And then a moment later her eyes will grow soft as she declares, "Of course, it was the most wonderful experience of my life!"

This jumble of joy and trauma can be traced back to the very first mother's experience. God said to Eve, "With pain you will give birth.…" But after Eve became Mom to the first baby, only astonishment and joy filled her birth announcement. She exclaimed, "With the help of the LORD I have brought forth a man" (Gen. 3:16, 4:1).

First, distress. Then, elation and wonder. And sometimes, more than a little anxiety.

Eve understood that she couldn't birth and raise a child except with the Lord's help. And we know that too. From the moment we first lay eyes on our baby—whether we gave her birth or God blessed us with her through the miracle of adoption—we're flooded with awe. This tiny, pinkish, wrinkled human being is completely helpless—and counting on us!

No wonder mothers make the best prayer warriors in God's kingdom. And no wonder that from the moment of conception, if not before, we offer up prayers for our baby's health, safety, future, and happiness.

Prayer is a part of our God-given urge to protect, care for, and shape the precious children He has given us. And yet, having a baby is also wearing, worrying, and just plain exhausting. That can make prayers (at least ones containing complete thoughts) hard to come by. Our conversations with God so easily dwindle from good intentions to disjointed fragments. What mom hasn't started a hundred prayers in the middle of the night—sleeping or squalling child in arms—only to get foggy or frazzled? Or had every impulse to pray during the day get pushed aside by distractions: *Dear Lord, thank You for darling Sarah. I really need to start the laundry...call the clinic...plan dinner...* At times every parent wonders, *Am I really praying—or just worrying out loud?*

Thank God that He is such a perfect conversationalist, even when we're not. Our heavenly Father hears the unspoken longings behind our halting words—especially the ones that simply cry, "*Abba!* Father!" (Rom. 8:15). And He promises to answer us for our good and for our baby's.

GOD'S PRAYER BOOK

God also gives us plenty of help as we pray. In many ways, the Bible is a ready-made prayer book for God's family. In the Bible we find people using the Word in their prayers often. Jewish families wore words of Scripture on their foreheads, wrote it on doorframes, and prayed it back to God in temple worship (Deut. 6:6-9). Jesus and His disciples sang the psalms together as part of morning and evening prayers. And at the moment of His greatest agony on the cross, Jesus cried out the words of a psalm—"My God, my God, why have you forsaken me?"

(Ps. 22:1). Christians through the ages have used the psalms as a prayer book, often setting the verses to rhythm and melody.

Praying the Bible is an ancient, God-pleasing way to both talk and listen to our Father. When we pray Scripture, we use God's own words to help express our feelings, worries, requests, and praises. And at the same time, we allow His words to speak His truth and His heart back to us.

Praying Scripture as you hold or rock your baby or as you think about him or her throughout the day is a practical way to follow Paul's advice to "let the word of Christ dwell in you richly" (Col. 3:16). And you receive practical benefits as well. You're better able to hear God speaking His heart and His will to you. You're reminded of what He has done in the past—and can still do. You get "unstuck" from mindless routines and refreshed in the midst of the most demanding days.

Best of all, when you pray the Bible, you pray expectantly. Jesus said, "If you remain in me and my words remain in you, ask whatever you wish, and it will be given you" (John 15:7). How well our Father understands a parent's heart! What prayers are more poignant than the ones we offer on our children's behalf? What praises are more passionate than those we lift to God when our hearts are full of mother-love?

One of Scripture's best-loved prayers is Mary's hymn of praise for her miracle pregnancy. She had gone to visit her cousin, Elizabeth, who was also pregnant. As soon as the women greeted each other, the Holy Spirit prompted Elizabeth to exclaim: "Blessed are you among women, and blessed is the child you will bear!" (Luke 1:42).

At those words, Mary broke into song:

> *My soul glorifies the Lord*
> *and my spirit rejoices in God my Savior,*
> *for he has been mindful*
> *of the humble state of his servant.*
> *From now on all generations will call me blessed,*
> *for the Mighty One has done great things for me—*
> *holy is his name.*

(Luke 1:46-49)

Every mom recognizes the elation and gratefulness in Mary's response. Her praises resonate with other scriptures, including several psalms and Hannah's prayer in 1 Samuel 2.

Mary's prayer, often called the Magnificat, is a beautiful example of how the Word itself can help us express our deepest emotions. However, the possibilities for praying Scripture can reach even further than letting psalms and prayers speak for us. In the prayers that follow you'll be praying the Bible for your baby through many different expressions. You will:

- PERSONALIZE A BIBLE PRAYER

  "May my spouse and I experience unity as we raise this child in Your ways. May others see Your love in our love!" (a request from the prayer of Jesus for His disciples, John 17:23).

- PERSONALIZE A BIBLE VERSE

  "Lord, sometimes I don't know what I'm supposed to ask for or even want for my baby. How I thank You that Your Spirit is praying for me right now!" (confession and thanks from Rom. 8:26).

- PERSONALIZE A BIBLE PROMISE OR TEACHING

    *"Lord, help my child to grow up learning self-control. So
    many kids these days seem as vulnerable to enemy influences as
    a city with broken-down walls"* (a request from Prov. 25:28).

- PERSONALIZE A BIBLE PROMISE AS A RESPONSE FROM GOD

    *You pray: "I feel like such a failure as a parent today. My
    heart is breaking, Lord."*

    *You hear God answer: "I have seen your ways, but I will
    heal you. I will guide and comfort you. Out of sorrow I will
    bring praise to your lips!"* (comfort from Isa. 57:18-19).

Praying the Bible doesn't give us some sort of magical power. A prayer isn't like a coin we insert in a vending machine that guarantees the same result every time. (What kind of relationship would that be?) None of us ever gets leverage on our heavenly Father or controls His actions, no matter how we pray. And yet, *prayer and power go together.* The Bible tells us we have access to power in Jesus' name (John 14:12-14), that there is power in the Word (Heb. 4:12), and that God will release His power through our faith (Mark 11:22-24).

Speaking of power, we never pray alone. We're actually joining with Christ in His greatest work in heaven today. The Bible says that He is our high priest who stands before the Father interceding for His children (Hebrews 7, Rom. 8:34)—that means us and our baby too. With our every heartfelt plea, His Spirit pleads for us (Rom. 8:26-27). We're not parenting Baby alone!

MAKING THESE PRAYERS YOUR OWN

You might think these suggestions are all about tidying up your language or your life so that God will hear you. Not so. Consider how many of David's psalms begin with a cry from the depths! The true test for any prayer is always the heart. What is our intention? We don't have to sound or feel better in order to approach our Father in humble trust.

Unlike the cashier at the grocery store, when God asks, "How are you today?" He really wants to know. God longs for honest communication with us—even during that hectic hour before dinner when we have only one nerve left and Baby is trying to cut another tooth on it. Even when we can't recall *one* Bible promise, much less pray it!

I encourage you to keep *Praying the Bible for Your Baby* on your nightstand or in the nursery and use it for daily spiritual refreshment. An easy-to-use index at the back of the book will help you track down a prayer by topic. Subjects are arranged under five felt-need categories like, "Lord, As a Mother I'm Feeling…" or "Lord, Bless My Baby's Future With…"

Your heavenly Father has intimate, moment-by-moment knowledge of your every need and feeling as a new parent. His parent-heart delights in your baby and carries him/her close to His heart (Isa. 40:11). My prayer is that the Holy Spirit will use this little book to encourage you and bring you even more joy during this blessed season of your life.

In Jesus' name I pray, and am confident, that the God who gives endurance, encouragement, and hope (Rom. 15:5,13) *will accomplish immeasurably more than all you can ask or imagine. How thankful I am that His power—the same power that raised Jesus from the dead* (1 Pet. 1:21)—*is at work in you, and your family, and in the baby you love so much* (Eph. 3:20)!

Pour out your heart like water
in the presence of the Lord.
Lift up your hands to him
for the lives of your children.

LAMENTATIONS 2:19

SWEET ANTICIPATION

Prayers for

Expectant Parents

Your Works Are Wonderful!

I praise you because I am fearfully and wonderfully made;
your works are wonderful, I know that full well.

PSALM 139:14

Dear God and Creator, You are amazing! I praise You because our child has been fearfully and wonderfully made. You've created our baby's inmost being and masterfully knit him together—tiny eyes, silky skin, fragile bones (Ps. 139:13). The scope of Your accomplishment is astounding, immeasurable, beyond our wildest imagination.

Even with the high-tech instruments of medicine, our baby remains hidden from us. But not from You (v. 15). You watch over this little being at every moment, even as You weave strands of DNA together and carefully select genes that will imprint our child with an utterly unique set of personal characteristics. And far beyond the reach of any micron telescope, You're shaping a chosen vessel, a spiritual being who'll one day learn to say, "Abba!"

How amazing it is that every day of this child's future has been written in Your book—before even one of them has come to be (v. 16)! Nothing about our baby will ever be a secret to You. Such knowledge is too wonderful for me, Lord (v. 6).

Thank You that no matter where my child may be from now on—whether in the dark cocoon of the womb or in the bright light of Your world—Your hand will continue to guide him and hold him securely (vv. 8-10).

Thank You, amazing Creator, awesome Lord—and Abba, Father!

In Your name I pray. Amen.

With the Lord's Help

Adam lay with his wife Eve, and she became pregnant and
gave birth to Cain. She said, "With the help of the LORD
I have brought forth a man."

GENESIS 4:1

Lord of creation, thank You for staying by Eve's side. The first
mother must have felt so alone, confused, and overwhelmed
during the first human pregnancy. But You stayed with her.
After Eve disobeyed You, failed her husband, and helped ruin
Your Garden, You stayed to help—all through the pain until
the joy.

Please stay with me. Be Lord of this, another creation day.
Breathe life into my womb! Only with Your help can I bring
forth a new human being!

Hear my mother-prayer, Lord: *With Your help,* let me
carry a healthy pregnancy to term. *With Your help,* let me

deliver a baby for Your glory…and my husband's pride…and my joy. *With Your help,* let me be a nurturing, gentle, strong mother every day that You give me this child to love.

I cry out with the psalmist: "Arise, LORD! Lift up your hand, O God. Do not forget the helpless" (Ps. 10:12).

Do not be afraid, O helpless daughter, My little one, for I Myself will help you (from Isa. 41:14).

Thank You, Lord! If You are my helper, I don't need to be afraid (Ps. 118:6).

I will never leave you or forsake you. You are Mine (from Deut. 31:6, Isa. 43:1).

Thank You, Lord of expectant mothers, Lord of my creation day. I worship You.

Amen.

Adopted into Love

She took him to Pharaoh's daughter and he became her
son. She named him Moses, saying,
"I drew him out of the water."

EXODUS 2:10

Heavenly Father, how we thank You for the miracle of adoption! We rejoice in the truth that, as with Moses, sometimes it is Your exact will and plan for one woman to give birth to a baby and allow another couple to parent it. In yet another way, even Your own Son Jesus was "adopted" by Joseph.

Thank You, Father, that You are not limited by the physical but are able to exceed all we would ask for or imagine (Eph. 3:20). Today I lift my heart and voice in thanksgiving for the baby who is on the way to our hearts and our home right now. We are "pregnant," Lord! And You have already given us an overwhelming love for this little life that we have waited for so long.

Continue to give us wisdom to understand Your will for us and Your destiny for our baby. May we always remember that we, too, have been adopted as Your children (Rom. 8:15,23). You have chosen us (1 Pet. 2:9), named us (Isa. 43:1), and made us full heirs of Your riches (Rom. 8:17). As we lavish love on this life about to enter ours, we will continually remember how great is the love You lavish on us (1 John 3:1)!

Amen.

A Good Name

The first to come out was red, and his whole body was like a hairy garment; so they named him Esau [meaning "hairy"]. After this, his brother came out, with his hand grasping Esau's heel; so he was named Jacob [meaning "grabber"].

GENESIS 25:25-26

Lord Jesus, name above all names, I can't even imagine naming my baby Hairy or Grabber! But as Baby's arrival draws near, everyone we know seems to have a different idea about what a "good" name is.

Wisely guide us, Lord, as we choose a name for our child. We want one that tells the truth about this little one, Your gift of life—his place in our hearts and his unique place in this world.

And help us, dear Lord, in the years ahead, to raise our child to have the kind of "good name" that really matters.

May our baby's name be always spoken fondly and with respect because of his good reputation (Prov. 22:1).

May our baby's name always be linked with Yours because he is one of Your people (2 Chron. 7:14). May he say as Jeremiah did, "I bear Your name" (Jer. 15:16).

May our baby's name be written forever in Your Book of Life (Phil. 4:3, Heb. 12:23, Rev. 21:27).

Lord Jesus, thank You that You hear the desires of our hearts for our baby. Thank You so much for giving us the heritage of those who hold Your name in awe (Ps. 61:5)!

Amen.

This Is the Miracle

Before you were conceived I wanted you.

Before you were born I loved you.

Before you were here an hour I would die for you.

This is the miracle of love.

MAUREEN HAWKINS

Heavy-Laden

Come to me, all you who are weary and burdened,
and I will give you rest.

MATTHEW 11:28

Heavenly Father, I come to You today, looking for the rest You promise. I have never felt more weary and heavy-laden. Now I understand David's lament: "I am poured out like water, and all my bones are out of joint" (Ps. 22:14).

Father, I had no idea that these nine months would be so hard. I can't remember what it feels like to not be pregnant, to feel energetic, to be comfortable. I want to cry out in my frustration and discomfort: "LORD, heal me, for my bones are in agony.… How long, O LORD, how long?" (Ps. 6:2-3).

Please grant me the grace to endure this perpetual physical turmoil. Keep my baby well. Where my body falls short of providing all the rest and nutrients he needs, please intervene and protect him. Others are praying for me, too, and Your Word says that prayers offered in faith will bring health to those in need (James 5:14-16). Thank You.

"Cast your burdens on the Lord and he will sustain you. He will never let his chosen ones down" (from Ps. 55:22).

I praise You for this promise, Lord. Even when I barely have the energy for it, I'll praise and thank You because You will keep giving me Your strength (2 Sam. 22:33, Ps. 59:17). You will keep renewing my soul and spirit (Isa. 40:29-31). You will never let me down.

Amen.

Prepare Our Hearts

Come, for everything is now ready.

LUKE 14:17

Lord Jesus, everything seems ready: soft sheets in the crib, changing table set up, rocking chair just so, nursery warm and welcoming…

But are we really ready, Lord? How easy it is to focus on all the externals. We want to be ready *in our hearts.*

Cleanse our hearts and renew our motives (Ps. 51:10). Fill us and our home with Your Holy Spirit (Eph. 5:18). Refresh our marriage to honor You and each other (Eph. 5:33). Anoint us with a sense of humor and a spirit of prayer (Rom. 12:12). Help us live by faith (Heb. 10:38). Open our eyes to the new (Isa. 43:18-19).

We want to be ready for Baby—and for all the "immeasurably more" that You have in store (Eph. 3:20).

In Your name we trust. Amen.

We are never prepared for what we expect.

JAMES A. MICHENER

The Best-Laid Plans

Many are the plans in a man's heart,
but it is the LORD's purpose that prevails.

PROVERBS 19:21

Lord, when we first dreamed of welcoming a child into the world, we thought circumstances would be different: our nest would be more cozy, our marriage more mature, our jobs more secure. Sometimes we wonder, *Could there be a worse time for Baby's arrival?*

Today we surrender the plans of our hearts to You. How stuck we can get in our own perspective!

But our steps are directed by *You,* King of our lives (Prov. 20:24)! And Your plan for us will stand the test of time (Ps. 33:11). You know our deepest wishes and concerns (Ps. 7:9). And You're always up to something wonderful for the ones You love (Rom. 8:28). Especially wonderful surprises!

Please forgive our doubts and help us to trust You with our imperfect circumstances and foiled "master plan." Help us to stop worrying about how things are "supposed" to be and start remembering who You are.

"No eye has seen, no ear has heard, no mind has conceived what God has prepared for those who love him" (1 Cor. 2:9).

"'I know the plans I have for you,' declares the LORD, 'plans to prosper you and not to harm you, plans to give you hope and a future'" (Jer. 29:11).

Yes, dear loving Lord, we can trust You with our plans and with our lives. And we can trust You with our baby.

Amen.

Father, I'm Afraid

To the woman he said, "I will greatly increase your pains in childbearing; with pain you will give birth to children."

GENESIS 3:16

Heavenly Father, this morning I agree with Job who declared, "How painful are honest words!" (Job 6:25). You—who are my comfort—are letting me know that pain is ahead. And I confess, Lord, that I am afraid of pain. Somehow, the idea of trying to focus on a spot on a wall while sucking down sourballs as my husband chants, "Choo… Chooo…" doesn't put me at ease.

Please, Lord, grant me the courage I need to be strong when the time comes. Hear my cry for mercy (Ps. 28:6).

Fear not, for I have redeemed you; I have called you by name. When you pass through the waters, I will be with you; and when you pass through the rivers, they will not sweep over you. For I am the LORD your God, your Savior. You are precious and honored in my sight, and I love you (from Isa. 43:1-4).

Thank You, Lord, for Your sweet, comforting, unfailing love. Nothing can separate me from it (Rom. 8:31-39)—not even thirty-six hours of labor.

While I focus on the wall and keep my breathing deep, let this be my secret mantra: "Your love…endures…forever…! Your love…endures…forever!" (from Ps. 118:2).

And thank You, Lord, for Your gift of new life that I will cradle in my arms on the other side of this pain.

Amen.

Courage is not simply one of the virtues,
but the form of every virtue at the testing point.

C. S. LEWIS

Perfect Timing

My times are in your hands.

PSALM 31:15

Dear Lord, I'm counting the days and the pounds and the centimeters and the Braxton Hicks and the new folded sleepers—but the real countdown never comes. When will it come, Lord? Every morning I wake up praying that this is the day. I'm counting the bumps (Baby must have fourteen elbows). I'm counting the last time I saw my toes…

Everyone tells me, "Baby will come when she's ready." But *I'm* ready, Lord! My restless mind wanders through Your Word. You say,…*warn those who are idle* (Baby's been so quiet lately), *encourage the timid* (is he afraid to face the world?), *help the weak* (maybe he's just not strong enough yet), *be patient with everyone* (even babies who are late?) (1 Thess. 5:14).

Okay, Lord. I know the apostle Paul didn't have babies in mind. But he might have if he'd ever been pregnant.

Let me hear from You today (I'm *so* pregnant). Your Word says that a wise woman doesn't fret but waits on Your timing with patience (Ps. 37:8). Help me, Lord, to stop counting. Help me to be at ease and to give You time to work.

Wait for the LORD; be strong and take heart and wait for the LORD (Ps. 27:14).

Lord, I'll wait for You. Give me grace to wait. Renew my strength in these days (Isa. 40:31). I'm confident in Your goodness, and I know I'll see it soon (Ps. 27:13).

Oh, let it be *soon!*

Amen.

Waiting is important work.

SUE MONK KIDD

The Longest Conversation

Pray in the Spirit on all occasions with all kinds of
prayers and requests. Be alert and always
keep on praying for all the saints.

EPHESIANS 6:18

Dear Heavenly Father, as I anticipate my baby's arrival, I feel a
new desire to pray earnestly and without ceasing. Is this part of
being a mother?

Please continue to turn every impulse and concern of my
mother-heart into conversation with You. Speak, Spirit, in me
and through me on "all occasions and with all kinds of prayers
and requests." Yes, Lord, that is what I want. Let my baby feel
my prayers even now.

In the days to come, Father, bless every hurried mumble
("Lord, help him sleep"), every anguished plea ("Oh, cool
his fever"), every intercession ("Lord, raise him up to be a

champion for You"), every dreamy request ("Bring him a wonderful Christian wife").

Teach me, like Daniel, to be faithful and regular in my praying—and always full of thanks (Dan. 6:10).

From every acorn of worry and self-centered concern, grow in my life a mighty oak of faith in what You can do. And what You can do is "immeasurably more than all we ask or imagine" (Eph. 3:20)!

And grant, Lord, that my child will grow up making prayer a priority in his life. May he exclaim like David, "My heart says of you, 'Seek his face!' Your face, LORD, I will seek" (Ps. 27:8).

Amen.

WELCOME, LITTLE ONE

*Prayers for Baby's
First Few Weeks*

Oh, the Tiniest Toes!

Come, let us bow down in worship,
let us kneel before the LORD our Maker.

PSALM 95:6

Dear Heavenly Father, our baby is Your special creation. We anticipated her for many months. But You have been anticipating her birth since before time began (Ps. 139:15-16). Now she's actually here, ready to begin her life and to begin to do Your will even before she can speak—while she yet gurgles and coos Your praises (Eph. 2:10).

No wonder she turned out so beautifully (how I love her tiny toes). Everything You imagine and shape is a wonder (Isa. 25:1)! How grateful I am that Your unchanging goodness will always surround our baby (Ps. 23:6).

Like the farthest star and tiniest flower at Creation, our child is the skilled, tender work of Your fingers (Ps. 139:13).

How You made our baby in the womb is beyond understanding (Eccles. 11:5).

You are the God who "forms the mountains [and] creates the wind" (Amos 4:13)—and You made our baby's ten tiny fingernails!

You are the God who "reveals his thoughts to man,...who turns dawn to darkness" (Amos 4:13)—and You put starlight in her twinkling button eyes!

You are the God who "treads the high places of the earth" (Amos 4:13)—and You, Almighty God, gave our child the softest feet!

To You, dear God, I bow in worship. O how excellent is Your name in all the earth (Ps. 8:1)!

Amen.

I remember leaving the hospital...thinking,
"Wait, are they going to let me just walk off with him?
I don't know beans about babies!"

ANNE TYLER

Family Resemblances

*And we, who with unveiled faces all reflect the Lord's
glory, are being transformed into his likeness.*

2 CORINTHIANS 3:18

God of wonder, she's here! She definitely has my eyes, her
father's mouth—and she's bald like Grandpa! And she's so
beautiful, Lord—perfect just the way she is. Thank You for
this miracle mosaic of family resemblances and first-on-the-
planet uniquenesses.

Lord, thank You for caring about beauty. May our baby's
beauty bring honor to You and grace to others her whole life.
Protect her body, soul, and spirit from every harm. Lift her up
by Your angels (Ps. 91:11).

As she grows up, may Your beautiful character glow from
her like a light (Eph. 5:8). May she radiate what Paul
described as "the fruit of the light...all goodness, righteousness
and truth" (Eph. 5:9-10). May her presence be prized because

she is quick to share the good news of Your saving love (Rom. 10:15). And by the artful hand of Your Holy Spirit, shape in her the lasting loveliness that comes from a gentle and quiet spirit (1 Pet. 3:4).

Lord, this is our Prayer of Family Resemblances: With each passing day, may we increasingly reflect Your glory as Your Spirit transforms us into the beautiful likeness of Christ (2 Cor. 3:18).

Amen.

There is only one pretty child in the world,
and every mother has it.

ENGLISH PROVERB

A Dedication Prayer

I will...present him before the LORD.

Lord of new life, just as Hannah prayed for Samuel, we have prayed for this child, and in Your mercy You've granted our request. Now we bring our baby before You, to give him back to You (1 Sam. 1:28). Everything comes from You—and we are giving You only what Your loving hand has given us (1 Chron. 29:14).

We not only dedicate our child but ourselves as well, in all humility. We ask You to grant us wisdom (James 1:5) to raise this precious gift of Your grace. May we always remember that he is a blessing from You, a reward and a heritage (Ps. 127:3), and not a burden.

We vow to raise him according to Your ways and not our own, teaching him from day one to seek You with all his heart and soul (Deut. 4:29). We promise to do our best to write

Your commandments on his heart (Deut. 6:7-8). We consecrate ourselves and our baby to You—and will wait in faith for You to do amazing things (Josh. 3:5).

Thank You, Lord, for choosing us as caretakers of this precious life. We say with the psalmist:

"How can I repay the LORD for all his goodness to me? I will lift up the cup of salvation and call on the name of the LORD. I will fulfill my vows to the LORD in the presence of all his people" (Ps. 116:12-14).

We dedicate our baby to You, confident not in ourselves, but in Your wonderful faithfulness (2 Tim. 2:13).

In Jesus' name we pray. Amen.

Thirsty Again

Whoever drinks the water I give him will never thirst.
Indeed, the water I give him will become in him
a spring of water welling up to eternal life.

JOHN 4:14

Heavenly Father, thank You for Your living water that satisfies our thirsty souls. I think about Your "spring of life" when I'm nursing. You know, Father, how much I love those private moments. But sometimes I wish I could offer my baby milk that would satisfy her forever.

Today I pray that each feeding time with Baby would remind me of You and of the water of life that You provide for us free of charge (Isa. 55:1). You satisfy the deepest needs and longings of Your children (Isa. 58:11). You cradle us in Your strong, everlasting arms (Deut. 33:27). Thank You that You don't just make Your gift available—You beg us to come and have our fill (Isa. 55:2).

Thank You, Father, that through faith in Your Son, Jesus, streams of living water will flow like a river from our souls to bless others around us (John 7:38). This is the kind of "eternal fullness" that I ask for my child.

But for today, and on behalf of my happily nursing baby, I thank You and praise You for mother's milk—so sweet and rich and full of mother-love.

In Jesus' name. Amen.

Unexpected Outcomes

*The LORD is close to the brokenhearted and
saves those who are crushed in spirit.*

PSALM 34:18

Father God, our baby is not the picture-perfect baby we
imagined she would be. The doctors make attempts at
optimism, loving friends at comfort. Yet we feel alone (and
even guilty) in our grief. What is Your plan for this blameless
baby, for us, for this unexpected outcome?

Spirit of God, should we pray for a miracle? For grace to
embrace the disappointment? For joy that we can't yet find?
Spirit, now more than ever we need You to pray for us
(Rom. 8:26-27). Your will eludes us. It's hard to see through
the tears. Our hearts are broken and our spirits are crushed.

Be close to us, Comforter, as You've promised. You draw
near when we pray to You (Deut. 4:7, Ps. 145:18). Come

quickly, Lord. We are poor and needy, and You are our help and deliverer (Ps. 40:17).

Lord, although we can't understand right now, we will cling to Your promises. You are faithful to every promise You make, and we know with our hearts and souls that not one of Your good promises has ever failed (Josh. 23:14). You have said You will deliver us from our troubles, and we trust You now (Ps. 72:12-13).

Dear God, You are loving and faithful toward everything You have made, even this baby who has elicited so much love and heartache (Ps. 145:9,13). How we long for the day when You will release us from our troubles so that we can go out with joy and peace (Isa. 55:12). Help us to wait on You in patience and confidence.

Amen.

A Newborn Scent

*We are to God the aroma of Christ
among those who are being saved.*

2 CORINTHIANS 2:15

Heavenly Father, today my baby smells of baby powder and of something mysteriously fresh and impossible to define. As I brush her cheek against mine and breathe in her heavenly scent, I also long to be a sweet aroma to You, Lord. Thank You that just as surely as my baby was born from the womb, I have been born again by Your Spirit (John 3:7-8). And in the same way I delight in holding Baby close, You delight in holding me close.

"The LORD takes delight in his people; he crowns the humble with salvation" (Ps. 149:4).

Thank You, Father, for loving me!

Amen.

Everlasting Arms

The eternal God is your refuge, and underneath
are the everlasting arms.

DEUTERONOMY 33:27

My Father, as I sit here holding my baby, that song keeps going
through my head: "He's got the whole world in his hands.…
He's got the itty bitty babies in his hands."

It's such a comforting thought, Lord. And yet, how can it
be? Are Your arms *really* big enough to hold the whole world?
Are they *really* everlasting? (What I'm really asking is, can I
trust You to pay close attention to my own "itty bitty" baby?)

Forgive my doubting, Lord. You've carried me this far, so
of course You can carry my baby whenever she needs You. I've
known firsthand how Your arms feel around me and how Your
right hand holds me fast when I would run toward danger
(Ps. 139:9-10). Why should I fear You'll let go now?

The hold I have on this precious life asleep in my arms is

fierce. But You've said that You will gather the lambs—and that means my lamb, too—in Your arms and carry them close to Your heart (Isa. 40:11).

Moses felt Your arms, too, when You carried the Israelites through the desert "as a father carries his son" (Deut. 1:31). As my father carried me. As I, in turn, carry my child. Close against my chest, cradled in my arms. How much more, Lord, will You hold on!

Help me loosen my fearful grip today. Help me to remember that Your grip is infinitely strong and Your arms everlasting. And as You hold my baby, You hold me too.

Amen.

The Mystery Revealed

We never know the love of a parent till we become parents ourselves.

When we first bend over the cradle of our own child,

God throws back the temple door

and reveals to us the sacredness and mystery

of a father's and mother's love to ourselves.

HENRY WARD BEECHER

Just a Little Advice

Listen to advice and accept instruction.

PROVERBS 19:20

Lord, I haven't asked for any, but it seems everyone wants to give me some advice on Baby! "Bathe him daily." "Don't bathe him daily." "Always feed an infant on demand." "Only feed on a strict schedule!"

Your Word tells me that there's safety in the counsel of many (Prov. 15:22). And You know I want the best for my baby. So I pray for ears that are willing to hear and a heart that is teachable. Show me, Lord, what advice to heed and what advice to let go. Thank You that my love for my baby will cover a multitude of mistakes I might make. Help me not to panic, and when I feel confused, may I remember the words used to advise Your kings: "First seek the counsel of the LORD!" (1 Kings 22:5, 2 Chron. 18:4).

Thank You, Father, that most of the people who offer unsolicited advice do so because they love me and my baby. Today I choose to lay down the kind of pride that resists advice and leads to quarrels (Prov. 13:10). Today, I will seek You first, and I will sing with the psalmist: "I will praise the LORD, who counsels me!" (Ps. 16:7).

Amen.

The Wisdom of Many

"The intelligent man is always open to new ideas.
In fact, he looks for them." (Proverbs 18:15, TLB)

Mom's translation:

"A smart mother lets others help with her new baby.
In fact, she even asks for advice!"

Sweet Hours of Peace

*Peace I leave with you; my peace I give you. I do not give
to you as the world gives. Do not let your hearts be troubled
and do not be afraid.*

JOHN 14:27

PRAYING PHILIPPIANS 4

Lord of peace, I rejoice in You, today. Tonight. Always. Yes, I'll
say it again for my own ears—and for my baby's too: I rejoice
continually in You! May this joyful confidence in You sweeten
my life, even in the long hours; may it quietly prepare me and
the ones I love for Your coming (vv. 4-5). I surrender my
worries and fears to You, Lord, especially those for my baby.
*Is he getting enough milk? Or too much? Why does he cry? Can he
feel my love?*

For every anxious thought I put down—for every diaper I

change, every cry I answer—I pick up a prayer of serene trust in You (v. 6).

I choose not to be anxious about my baby's health, safety, or even my own weaknesses as a mother. But instead I trust in Your tender care. Thank You so much for Your peace—a miracle completely beyond my understanding—which guards my heart and mind each day (vv. 6-7).

Amen.

Holy Hands

Do not be afraid, but let your hands be strong.

ZECHARIAH 8:13

Father, such tiny hands! So fragile, so delicate. How I love these miniature fingers clasped around mine. What will they grow to accomplish? Will my baby grow up using them for good? I pray they won't ever be used for evil!

How I long for my baby to grow up strong, diligent, and eager to work (Prov. 10:4). May his hands always be busy looking for ways to help others (Eccles. 11:6, Eph. 2:10).

Such tiny hands—with such great potential! May their touch bring healing and hope to many, as though they were the hands of Christ (Acts 3:6-7).

Give my baby holy hands, that he may lift them to You in worship and service (1 Tim. 2:8) and use them as tools for good (Rom. 6:13).

Touch his hands with Your mercy, that he may show mercy to others. Touch his hands with Your grace, that he may in turn be gracious. Touch his hands with Your love, that he will respond one day by lifting them up to You in surrender.

Such tiny hands! On their behalf and for Your glory, I pray this in Jesus' name.

Amen.

A Mother's Psalm 23

Lord, You are my baby's lifelong keeper.

You will provide for all his needs, and mine as well (v. 1).

You gently lay him down on flannel sheets and gently lead him into sweet dreams (v. 2).

You keep restoring my soul for both our sakes so that when my baby wakes again, I am glad (v. 3).

Even when my baby suffers because of sickness, teething, and earaches, he won't need to fear anything—and neither will I—for You will always be near. With Your night songs and God-hugs, You will comfort us (v. 4).

Lord, You prepare a place of peace for us in the darkest morning hours. You watch me anoint my baby with lotion and powder (v. 5).

You hear each sleepy prayer and blessing in Your name. Lord, You know when I smile at Baby, how laughter spills out of my heart (vv. 5-6).

I'm confident that Your goodness and mercy will follow him all the sweet days of his life. And my baby will dwell in Your house of love forever (v. 6).

Amen.

BABY DAZE

Prayers for Long Nights

and Busy Days

Grubby Love

Whatever you do, work at it with all your heart,
as working for the Lord.

COLOSSIANS 3:23

Heavenly Father, You ask me to work with all my heart at whatever I do. But what I do is launder bibs, receiving blankets, and assorted *oops*es all day. I scrub out bottles. I clean up messy little bottoms. Can You receive these grubby tasks as gifts for Your glory?

I thought motherhood would be more about bonnets and peach pies and lullabies and sheets that smelled of prairie sunshine.

You know I love my baby, Lord. But my work is downright messy. And I feel messy all the time. Is there spit-up on my blouse? Can my husband smell his lover's Donna Karran perfume over the smell of his baby's Desitin ointment?

You know I love You, Lord. Please, give me grace to get grubby.

Jesus, having loved his own, now showed them the full extent of his love. He got up from the meal, took off his outer clothing, and wrapped a towel around his waist. After that, he poured water into a basin and began to wash his disciples' feet, drying them with the towel that was wrapped around him (from John 13:1-5).

Thank You, Lord Jesus. Let me exalt You all day in my heart (Ps. 92:1-2) with rag and powder and soap.

Now that you know these things, you will be blessed if you do them (John 13:17).

Amen.

Wee Hours

*My eyes stay open through the watches of the night,
that I may meditate on your promises.*

PSALM 119:148

Father, the house is filled with hush. Only a creak here, a hum there. In these wee hours when everyone sleeps, silence wraps me like fleece. Just my baby and I keep watch. And You keep watch with us, Father.

What a comfort to know You never sleep—or need to (Ps. 121:4). But I drift in and out, exhausted. Let me drift tonight, safe in Your comforting presence. Just help me stay alert enough to nurse Baby, not her teddy bear. And help me listen for Your voice.

Yes, Lord, at least these wee hours are private. At least the distractions are few. So with Samuel, I whisper into the darkness, "Speak, LORD, for your servant is listening" (1 Sam. 3:9).

Clear my mind. Counsel and instruct me, even at night (Ps. 16:7). What is it You want to say? I strain to hear...

This is what I hear tonight: I hear Your love song for me and my baby (Ps. 42:8). Your love song falls on my spirit soft as Baby's breath on my skin. Its music fills my inner being with joy and rest (Exod. 33:14).

And I sing it back to You, a sleepy prayer of praise to the God of my life (Ps. 42:8).

Amen, Lord Jesus.

Sleepless in Heaven

"He is always watching, never sleeping." (Ps. 121:4, TLB)

Mom's translation:

"Alas, God and baby share the same clock:

Neither slumber nor sleep!"

Jesus, Did You Ever...?

*For we do not have a high priest who is unable
to sympathize with our weaknesses.*

HEBREWS 4:15

Jesus, Son of Mary, today I'm wondering: Did you ever eat
bugs? Did you cry when it thundered or when a crowd
clapped? Pull yourself up on the living room furniture—and
topple everything over? Turn your little face up to Mary and
laugh when You should have been nursing? Smash jelly
sandwiches in Your hair?

Jesus, Son of God, how comforting that You know what it
is to be human. You've been a baby boy and a grown-up
man—tested in every way—yet You never sinned (Heb. 4:15).
You are able to respond gently and compassionately to me
when I'm ignorant (when I don't know what weird rashes
mean) or go astray (almost every day) (Heb. 4:16). Thank You!

Jesus, Lord of my home, You know me and You know my

baby (Jer. 12:3). That's why I rejoice that You are now our great high priest (Heb. 4:14) and my baby's ceaseless intercessor before Your Father's throne. Because of You, I can rest easy, knowing that he will receive mercy and find grace to help in his time of need (Heb. 4:16). Like when he eats a bug.

In Your name I pray. Amen.

The Most Excellent Way

The greatest…is love.

1 CORINTHIANS 13:13

PRAYING 1 CORINTHIANS 13:1-8

Heavenly Father, today remind me from Your Word about the most excellent way of love.

If I gurgle and coo and engage my baby in unintelligible conversation but don't love this precious child, then I am only a silly, baby-doting woman (v. 1).

If I know everything about child raising and am looked up to as an "expert" but don't parent with love, then all my knowledge is good for nothing (v. 2).

If I make all kinds of sacrifices for my child but do so out of selfish motives rather than out of God-directed love, then I will gain nothing (v. 3).

Love is patient with babies who won't burp, and it is kind

to babies who accidentally bite at breasts. It doesn't envy Mrs. Smith's baby or take too much pride in my baby's attempts to walk at nine months (v. 4).

Love doesn't ignore my baby's cries for help, isn't angered by lost binkies, and doesn't keep track of silk blouses destroyed by spit-up (v. 5). It always protects, always trusts, always hopes, always perseveres—even through the toughest days and nights (v. 7).

Where there are experts, they will change their opinions; where there are many words, they will run out; where there is certainty, it will give rise to doubts. But love...love never fails (v. 8)!

Thank You, Lord of love. Teach me this most excellent way.

I pray in Your name. Amen.

Angel Camp

*See, I am sending an angel ahead of you to guard you along
the way and to bring you to the place I have prepared.*

EXODUS 23:20

Loving Father, the bright-eyed duck and the button-nosed bear
watch patiently as Baby sleeps. But today let them remind me:
God's own angels watch over my little one.

Thank You, powerful God, that You have sent Your
"ministering spirits...to serve those who will inherit salvation"
(Heb. 1:14). Where others see a nursery, I see my child's
"Angel Camp." Yes, this place is owned and occupied by You,
Father. Your angel warriors stand watch here day and night to
deliver us, because we belong to You (Ps. 34:7). Thank You,
ever-present, ever-loving Lord!

Receive my worship now, God of this nursery. Let this
beautiful child be my gift to You. Let my heart of devotion be

my song of praise for You. Let this little room, with all its sweet sights and sounds and smells, be a temple where You are pleased to dwell.

Lord, You and Your angels are always welcome here!

Amen.

I Thought I Knew

> *Trust in the LORD with all your heart*
> *and lean not on your own understanding.*
>
> PROVERBS 3:5

Lord of wisdom, how I need you today! I thought I knew all about having a baby. But it was much simpler when this child was still just a plan. And my plan was perfect. You heard me proudly announce, "*My* baby's going to be on *my* schedule!" and, "No baby of mine's going to use a pacifier!"

Lord, Your sweetest gift of motherhood has brought some bittersweet humbling into my life. I accept this as from Your loving hand. Forgive my stupid arrogance.

I guide the humble in what is right and teach them my way (from Ps. 25:9).

Lord, guide me today—through Your Word, through Your Spirit, through the people You bring into my life. Thank You that You promise to provide wisdom without making me feel embarrassed for asking (James 1:5).

And now I'm asking with all my heart. It's You I trust, not how much I think I know (Prov. 3:5).

Amen.

Don't Worry, Just Ask

*Do not be anxious about anything, but in everything, by prayer
and petition, with thanksgiving, present your requests to God.*

PHILIPPIANS 4:6

Heavenly Father, thank You for inviting us to ask You for anything in Your own Son's name. Today, we will meditate on
Your promises.

We will not worry, saying, "What shall Baby eat?" or
"What shall those of us who can't nurse give Baby to drink?"
Our heavenly Father knows what we need (from Matt.
6:31-32).

God is able to meet all of my family's needs. His re-
sources—available to us through Christ Jesus—are limitless
(from Phil. 4:19)!

In Christ's precious name we pray. Amen.

"We're Rich!"

"The Lord's blessing is our greatest wealth." (Prov. 10:22, TLB)

Mom's translation:

"A new baby makes us even richer than we were before we

had to buy all those diapers."

Passing Storms

Cast all your anxiety on him because he cares for you.

1 PETER 5:7

Heavenly Lord, I know You care for me. And right now I need
to take You at Your word and cast all my anxiety on You. But,
oh Father, there's a lot!

Help! I don't know what to do! This baby's driving me
crazy with her constant whining and fussing.

Do not fret—it leads only to evil (Ps. 37:8).

Yes, Lord, that's what I wish my baby could understand.
And the evil it's leading to is my own anger! I'm cooped up
here with no escape. Someone is going to find me huddled in
a corner with cotton balls stuck in my ears.

Be still before the LORD and wait patiently for Me (from
Ps. 37:7).

Still? How can I be still when my baby's crying? In my

house, and in my heart, a storm is raging. Please answer my call. I am Your child.

In quietness and trust is your strength (Isa. 30:15).

Lord, teach me Your ways. Teach me quietness and trust. I can't calm my baby if I'm not calm. Help me to be quiet in my own spirit even as Baby is wailing. Is that possible?

Yes, Lord, I remember—You calmed a great storm with just one word. You can calm me now (Matt. 8:26). With open hands and a willing heart, I receive Your peace. I want Your mysterious and powerful calm to reign here, dear God (Phil. 4:7, Col. 3:15).

And as You quiet me, Lord, show me how to be as patient with my baby's passing storms and tears as You are with mine! By Your grace I pray these things.

Amen.

Kiss It Away

"A gentle answer turns away wrath." (Prov. 15:1)

Mom's translation:

"A mother's gentle kiss soothes her baby's hot tears."

The Great Physician

*Seeing Jesus, [Jairus] fell at his feet and pleaded earnestly
with him, "My little daughter is dying. Please come and put
your hands on her so that she will be healed and live."
So Jesus went with him.*

MARK 5:22-24

Dear Lord, my little child—the one You love—is sick (John
11:3). Come quickly, as You did for Jairus. Come with life-
giving power, as You did for Mary and Martha. Come to my
house today! Yes, come into her room. Touch her and save her
with Your power, healing Lord! I'm helpless and heartbroken
with concern. But You are God. You can make her well (John
14:13-14).

You feel the pain of a child's little miseries or huge health
challenges (1 Pet. 5:7). You cry when ones You love face
illness and grief (John 11:33-36). Thank You, compassionate
Lord, that You spent so much time healing people when You

were here (Matt. 9:35). I know You can do the same for my baby.

O Great Physician, You ask me simply to pray in faith for healing (Mark 5:34, James 5:15). Right now, I do. You can heal with one touch, one word. I believe—and I know Your power reaches far beyond where my belief ends (Mark 9:24).

That's why I can pray with praise, even before I know the outcome (Jer. 17:14).

I pray in Your powerful, healing name. Amen.

Heartwork

God sends children for another purpose

than merely to keep up the race—

(it is) to enlarge our hearts, to make us unselfish,

and full of kindly sympathies and affections.

MARY HOWITT

Gurgles of Praise

From the lips of children and infants you have ordained praise.

PSALM 8:2

Lord, I think I need an interpreter here: *Ga da do too. Ga da do too.* She's determined that it means something, but I just don't know what. I know that *Ba ba ba* means "mom"; *da* is easily discernible as "dad." But this new phrase has me stumped. Maybe it's baby talk for "hallelujah"? Infant-speak for "Praise the Lord"?

One thing's certain: I know *You* understand my baby's frustrated attempts at words. What a precious time this is, to hear her speak! I can't wait for her first "real" sentence. Our first "real" conversation. To hear her say "Jesus," and someday, "From birth I have relied on you; you brought me forth from my mother's womb. I will ever praise you" (Ps. 71:6).

As she grows, may her words be always "aptly spoken… like apples of gold in settings of silver" (Prov. 25:11)—

gracious, encouraging, healing, and seasoned with salt. How I long for her words to be pleasing to You! A fountain of blessing and a treasury of insight, wisdom, and grace.

Help me to be an example, Lord, for I know she'll repeat whatever she hears at home. For this reason, may the words of *my* mouth and the meditation of *my* heart be pleasing in Your sight (Ps. 19:14).

"As for me, I will always have hope; I will praise you more and more. My mouth will tell of your righteousness, of your salvation all day long, though I know not its measure" (Ps. 71:14-15).

Amen.

Boundless Love

Who shall separate us from the love of Christ?

ROMANS 8:35

Heavenly Father, today we thank You that nothing can separate our baby from Your love. Your love gives us hope as parents. Without Your love, we're not sure we'd even want to bring a baby into this world. But Your love is boundless, perfect, unfailing. Because of it, we can exclaim like the apostle Paul that nothing, *absolutely nothing,* can come between our child and Your love:

Neither death nor life,

(no accident, illness, chronic condition, or teething pain)

neither angels nor demons,

(no nightmare, boogey man, or any kind of evil influence)

neither the present nor the future,

(no nagging worry or looming crisis;

no predictable uncertainty or hypothetical impossibility)

nor any powers,

(no unsafe stranger, untrustworthy relative,

or uninvited government agency)

neither height nor depth,

(no unguarded stairwell or abandoned well shaft;

no giddy giggling or inconsolable sobbing)

nor anything else in all creation,

(no tornado or slippery tub; no long, hot car ride to Toledo;

no unsupervised snack of Lego, houseplant, or dog biscuit)

will be able to separate our baby

from the love of God that is in Christ Jesus our Lord!

(from Rom. 8:38-39)

Amen!

My Name Is Mommy

Prayers for a Whole
New Way of Life

My Name Is Mommy

*You will be called by a new name that the mouth
of the LORD will bestow.*

ISAIAH 62:2

Lord, how I love this new name You've given me—"Mommy"!
Is this the name for me that You've written upon the palms of
your hands (Isa. 49:16)?

What an awesome honor to be called Mommy—caretaker,
nurturer, teacher, comforter, example of faith. My greatest joy
lies in this name. But so do my greatest fears, Father. What if I
can't live up to it?

My only hope is knowing that You "gently lead those that
have young" (Isa. 40:11). That means me.

May I lean wholly on Your name as You enable me to live
up to mine.

Amen.

In Praise of Friends

Carry each other's burdens, and in this way
you will fulfill the law of Christ.

GALATIANS 6:2

Dear Lord Jesus, thank You for friends! How could I survive
without my buddies in the "Stroller Brigade"? What a comfort
to know others who carry a diaper bag for a purse and speak
the same language ("Go bye-bye." "Look at the moo-moos!").
Thank You, Lord, for someone I can call at 7 A.M., knowing
that she, too, has been up for hours.

And Lord, I'm so grateful for the godly, experienced moms
who serve as my examples and teachers (Titus 2:3-5). Just
knowing that they survived colicky days and sleep-deprived
nights with their babies gives me hope. What comfort I find
just in hearing their voices, seeing their smiles! How true is
Your Word when it says, "the pleasantness of one's friend
springs from [her] earnest counsel" (Prov. 27:9).

Most of all, thank You, Lord Jesus, for being my eternal friend. You are always with me, even in the quiet hours of the night (Ps. 121:3). You talk to me and counsel me from the pages of Your Word (James 1:5). You continually provide for my needs in ways I can't even imagine (Eph. 3:19-20).

Dear Friend of this mother and baby, it is in Your name I pray.

Amen.

A Great Big God

His greatness no one can fathom.

PSALM 145:3

Lord of heaven and earth, You created this entire universe, including billions of stars for babies to gaze at. But Lord, "When I consider your heavens, the work of your fingers...who am I that you should care for me?" (from Ps. 8:3-4). Or for my little one?

But You do care, Lord. When I don't know what to do about ear infections or when to say "no, no," You will grant wisdom (James 1:5). When I'm filled with insecurity, You promise to be my confidence (Prov. 3:26). When I fall, You will lift me up (Ps. 145:14)!

Thank You, Lord, for being big enough to make this whole wide wonderful world—but not too big to care for and watch over all of us who love You (Ps. 145:20).

Amen.

God's Children

The Spirit himself testifies with our spirit
that we are God's children.

ROMANS 8:16

Heavenly Father, how grateful I am to know that my baby is also Yours. Today, I meditate on Your promises:

"How great is the love the Father has lavished on
_____, that he/she should be called a child of God!
And that is what he/she is!"
(from 1 John 3:1)

"Yet to all who received him, including _____,
to those who believed in his name, he gave the right to
become children of God."
(from John 1:12)

In Your Son's name. Amen.

Nightgown Days

*And whatever you do, whether in word or deed, do it all
in the name of the Lord Jesus, giving thanks
to God the Father through him.*

COLOSSIANS 3:17

Lord, so often I'm still in my nightgown at noon. And except
for washing a few bottles, the only thing I have to show by the
end of most days is a dent in the couch where I sat holding
Baby as he fussed.

Lord, You say there's a season for every activity under
heaven (Eccles. 3:1). Maybe this is just my time for sitting on
the couch? Help me to remember that whatever I do—
including what I do with Baby—can be done unto You (Col.
3:17). And even the simplest activity done in Your name
counts for eternity. Surely this is one of the good works You've
prepared in advance for me to do (Eph. 2:10).

As I'm forced to do less busywork and more sitting, let my

thoughts be on You, Father. "Let the morning bring me word of your unfailing love, for I have put my trust in you" (Ps. 143:8). Help me to make good use of this time in my life when everything has somehow both slowed down and sped up.

As the dent in the couch gets deeper, may my time spent snuggling Baby be my holy act of worship to You. And as You look down from heaven to see if there are any who seek You (Ps. 14:2), I pray that You would see me. (Forgive the nightgown, Father—I dress for the job.)

In Your precious name I pray. Amen.

Can a Mother Forget?

*Can a mother forget the baby at her breast and
have no compassion on the child she has borne?
Though she may forget, I will not forget you!*

Lord of compassion, thank You for loving me as a mother loves
her baby! I can't think of any stronger image of intimacy and
devotion than a nursing mother. By making me a mother, You
have given me a chance to experience a whole new kind of
love for another human being—and a whole new context for
understanding Your love for me.

When I think of Jesus, whom You loved more than I love
my own baby, and how You gave Him up for us (John
3:16)…such love is too much for me to take in!

It's true! You will *not* forget me. And may I never forget
You, Lord.

Amen.

What Happened to My Body?

The body that is sown is perishable, it is raised imperishable.

1 CORINTHIANS 15:42

Father, what happened? I have hips the size of Kansas, a stomach that sags toward the floor, and a miniature human being attached permanently to my breast! And these stretch marks—they're like a road map of Chicago crisscrossing my belly and thighs.

Somehow, I don't feel so fearfully and wonderfully made anymore (Ps. 139:14). But I know that it's wrong for me to question what You have made, Lord (Isa. 45:9). Forgive me!

I do thank You, Father, that though it's hard to believe now, my body won't always be like this. (Oh, please, don't let it stay like this!) As I hold my baby to my breast, I know that every bulge, every extra inch, helped produce this precious gift.

So I present to You, Lord, this out-of-shape body as a living sacrifice. For You say this is my spiritual act of worship and one that's holy and pleasing to You (Rom. 12:1). Help me to be patient, to take care of my body's recovery as best I can, and to remember that my spirit is what really matters.

Today I will remember Your precious words: "Charm is deceptive, and beauty is fleeting; but a woman who fears the LORD is to be praised" (Prov. 31:30).

Amen.

Doxology for Baby

To the only God our Savior be glory, majesty, power and authority,
through Jesus Christ our Lord, before all ages, now and forevermore!

JUDE 25

PRAYING FROM JUDE 24 AND 25

Almighty Lord, on behalf of my baby, I offer a hymn of praise:

To You who are not only able, but oh so willing, to keep my baby from falling from Your care, I bring worship.

To You who will present my baby before Your glorious presence without fault and with great joy, I offer praise.

To You who are her God and Savior with every baby step of faith, with every babbled syllable of praise, I bring glory!

To You who are my baby's Lord of lords and King of kings, I ascribe all majesty and power!

To You who have the power and the love to one day bring my baby into Your eternal presence, I bow.

Amen.

Will Cry for Food

*I am the bread of life. He who comes to me will never go
hungry, and he who believes in me will never be thirsty.*

JOHN 6:35

Loving Father, my baby's hungry cries remind me of how I feel
when I'm hungry for Your Spirit. Help me to cry out in such
innocence to You, knowing You will gladly meet my needs.

Thank You, Bread of Heaven, for stilling the hunger of
those You cherish (Ps. 17:14) and for satisfying Your children
with good things (Ps. 107:9). How glad I am that You
promised us a food that satisfies the most raging hunger, a
food that lasts not just a couple of hours, but to eternal life
(John 6:27).

May my baby grow up with an appetite for You and for
Your Word that exceeds his desire for all else.

In Your name I pray. Amen.

A mother finds out what is meant by spitting image
when she tries to feed cereal to her baby.

IMOGENE FEY

I Used to Be Somebody

For we know...that he has chosen you.

1 THESSALONIANS 1:4

Father, I used to be somebody. But now...I don't feel important anymore. Sometimes I wonder if what I do even makes a difference. If I had a business card to hand out, it would say, "Somebody's mother. Changer of diapers. Wiper of spit."

Yet You see me, Lord, just as You saw Hagar crying in the desert (Genesis 16). You know me (Ps. 139:1), and You say I am made in Your image (Gen. 1:26-27). I am Your child if I believe in You (John 1:12).

You say in Your Word that I'm Your workmanship, created to do Your good deeds (Eph. 2:10) and chosen to bear You fruit (John 15:16). I am a dwelling place for Your Spirit (1 Cor. 3:16), holy and dearly loved (Col. 3:12).

When I consider all of that (and more), my groanings of

insignificance are silenced. You've chosen me for this invaluable position: loving mother of a human being! You've stooped from heaven to make me great (Ps. 18:35) and have given me a crown that will last forever (1 Cor. 9:25). Thank You, Lord.

Amen.

Husband of Mine

Where has your lover gone, most beautiful of women? Which
way did your lover turn, that we may look for him with you?

Lord of relationships, now that this baby has entered our lives, I
seem to have misplaced my husband! Or is he simply hiding
from me, now that my entire vocabulary consists of: "Diaper
her, feed her, burp her, put her in her crib"?

Lord, I used to long for romance—now I long for sleep.
To be honest, sometimes I see my husband as little more than
a baby-sitter so I can get errands done.

Your Word tells me, "Marriage should be honored by all"
(Heb. 13:4). Forgive me when I fail to honor my husband
with my time and affection, Father. I want to bring my
husband good, not harm, all the days of my life (Prov. 31:12).
But way beyond this, I don't want us ever to become married
strangers. I want our love affair to burn bright. How much

better for Baby to grow up in a home where parents say to each other, "I am my lover's and my lover is mine" (Song of Songs 6:3).

Thank You for the romantic love that led to our baby in the first place, Lord. May we honor that love and treasure it as much as You do.

Amen.

The Unquenchable Flame

For love is as strong as death,

its jealousy unyielding as the grave.

It burns like a blazing fire,

like a mighty flame.

Many waters cannot quench love;

rivers cannot wash it away.

SONG OF SONGS 8:6-7

A Real Mom

Her children arise and call her blessed.

PROVERBS 31:28

Lord of families, I think I'm actually becoming a real mom. I used to be well-groomed enough to appear in public by 9 A.M. Now I consider any day I can brush my teeth and my hair before noon to be a good day!

This is the day the LORD has made; let us rejoice and be glad in it (Ps. 118:24).

I used to worry about buying the right brand of formula. Now I automatically lick the salt off a french fry before handing it to Baby to eat.

She provides food for her family (Prov. 31:15).

I used to dream of romantic weekends away with my husband. Now my wildest, madcap fantasy is a nap.

When you lie down, your sleep will be sweet (Prov. 3:24).

I used to wonder what my baby really wanted. Now I know that "Blah glah gloo" means, "I'm bored sitting in this walker, and I really want to chew on the cat."

The breath of the Almighty gives understanding (from Job 32:8).

I used to make two trips to the car, but now I can fit a baby, a diaper bag, and a fold-up playpen all on one hip.

Offer the parts of your body to God as instruments of righteousness (from Rom. 6:13).

I used to hope for more money and an occasional cruise, but now I can't imagine my life being any richer.

Sons are a heritage from the LORD, children a reward from him (Ps. 127:3).

Today I thank You, Lord, for making me a real mom! Amen.

Back to Work?

Show me the way I should go, for to you I lift up my soul.

PSALM 143:8

Heavenly Father, I need Your help today as I consider whether or not to return to work outside my home. I feel my heart might break from conflicting emotions: the longing to be with my child every hour of the day; the reality of needing income; the uncertainty of what's best for my child and family.

I don't want to make this choice lightly or without prayer. I can hide nothing from You; Your Word judges my heart (Heb. 4:12-13). And so I pray with the psalmist, "Teach me to do your will, for you are my God; may your good Spirit lead me on level ground" (Ps. 143:10).

In the meantime, in whatever I do, both as a mother and employee, I will seek to work excellently, because I am serving You (Col. 3:23). I will work eagerly and with vigorous hands, and if You lead me back into the workplace,

I will put my earnings to use for my family's benefit (Prov. 31:16-17).

Lord, You know how much I long to be worthy of my husband's and child's blessing and praise (Prov. 31:28). I love my family more than any job or career, and I will seek to serve them and You with the purest of hearts. But I also know that if I lean on my own understanding, I will probably fail. And so today I choose to acknowledge Your lordship in every area of my life, knowing that You alone can guide my steps the right way (Prov. 3:5-6).

Thank You, Lord, for Your promise of unfailing wisdom (James 1:5)!

Amen.

Let Me Love Like You

God is love.

1 JOHN 4:16

PRAYING FROM 1 JOHN 4

Lord of love, You showed us how much You loved us when You sent Your Son to die for us (v. 9). Your kindness cost You.

When I'm awakened every hour through the night, and Baby is still unhappy, and Daddy is still sleeping like a log…let me love like You.

Lord of love, You didn't wait for us to come to You or to earn Your love. You made the first move to love so that we could understand and respond (v. 19). And this is how I want to love my family—like a mother bird who plucks her own softest feathers in order to make her baby's nest. Let me love like You.

Lord of love, Your love is perfect because it inspires no

fear—but only honor and respect (v. 18). When I'm feeling short-tempered with my baby, Father, and I feel the urge to hurt and punish rather than gently teach or discipline…let me love like You.

Lord of love, You are not partial to certain people, and You ask us to be willing to love all those You made as much as we love You (v. 20). When I'm suffering from comparisons and competitions with other mothers' Gerber-perfect babies, or I'm tempted to favor my own child above others…let me love like You, Lord.

Amen.

I ONLY
BLINKED

Prayers for
Baby's Future

Heaven Help Us

*O Lord, I beg you, let the man of God you sent to us come
again to teach us how to bring up the boy who is to be born.*

THE PRAYER OF SAMSON'S FATHER, JUDGES 13:8

A FATHER'S PRAYER

Heavenly Father, I cradle Your gift close to my heart—pink
skin on my hairy, sunburned arm, shiny trusting button eyes
looking up at…Dad. My son's playful, jerky little hand reaches
out…for what? What future waits for our miracle child, Lord?
And what help can his dad provide?

"I beg You" as Samson's father did, Lord. Teach me how
to be a father. You have only good in store for my baby
(Ps. 145:9)—but life is hard, and I'm so ordinary. Let Your
anointing never leave my son, and may he never leave You
(1 John 2:20). Make him mighty in Your kingdom. And
"come again"—every day—to make this dad mighty for You.

Amen.

I Blinked, and She Changed!

*Teach us to number our days aright,
that we may gain a heart of wisdom.*

PSALM 90:12

Heavenly Father, wasn't it just last week that I brought Baby home from the hospital, dwarfed in an oversized sleeper? Wasn't it yesterday that she pursed her lips and smiled at me for the first time? I remember the first time she turned her head toward me and smiled when I came into the room…

She's growing so fast—too fast, Lord! She's changing, and I'll never have these moments back.

Your Word reminds me that life is a mist, a vapor that appears for a little while and then vanishes (James 4:14). And You say that there is a time for everything in our lives (Eccles. 3:1). But oh how I wish these times with Baby could last and last!

Help me to be like Mary, who saved up all her moments with Baby Jesus and later savored them lovingly (Luke 2:19). Teach me Mary's mother-wisdom—to gather well and ponder well my baby's gifts!

The dust and the dishes will go on for years, but the first time she waves "bye-bye" will pass before I blink. Teach me, Lord, to save and celebrate with a grateful heart every Baby moment!

Amen.

Ready, Set, Plop!

> *I have no greater joy than to hear that my children
> are walking in the truth.*
>
> 3 JOHN 4

Father God, thank You for the precious gift of watching Baby try to crawl! I've been watching him for what seems like hours. One knee, the other knee, the bottom goes over, *plop!* Up again, he starts all over—then another *plop!*

Father, thank You for the amazing urges that my baby has to stand, to walk, to run. Bless and direct this "motion notion" in my baby his whole life long—in his body and in his spirit.

As my baby learns to stand upright on his chunky little legs, may he also learn to stand firm in his faith, not wavering or turning back (1 Cor. 16:13, James 1:6, Heb. 11:39). When danger threatens, may he say, "God keeps me safe on the heights" (Ps. 18:33).

When my baby can walk, shine Your light on his path

(Ps. 18:28). Make Your Word alive and active in his life to keep his way pure (Ps. 119:11, Heb. 4:12). Help him to walk in the narrow, right road because he wants to please You and receive Your blessing (Ps. 1:1, Matt. 7:14). Bring him friends to travel with him "in the footsteps of the faith" (Rom. 4:12). And when he walks through the fire, rescue him, Lord, as You've promised (Isa. 43:2).

And someday soon, when my baby can run, save him from too many tumbles. Thank You that Your everlasting arms will always be there when he falls (Deut. 33:27). May he always race to You—when he's in trouble, and when he's not (Ps. 119:32). And show him how to run with perseverance his race of faith (Heb. 12:1, 1 Cor. 9:24).

Oh, but I'm racing ahead of myself! Today he's just a baby, rocking on his knees, putting one in front of the other. *Plop!* And I praise You for the promise of that sound!

Amen.

Baby Armor

*Put on the full armor of God so that you can take
your stand against the devil's schemes.*

EPHESIANS 6:11

Lord, when I read these words of Yours, I shudder to think of
my baby having to stand up to Satan. Do spiritual suits of
armor come in baby size?

At such a young age, my baby hasn't yet been touched by
the sin of this world, and as her parent, my first impulse is to
shield her from the reality of evil. Help me instead, Father, to
equip her to cope victoriously with evil forces.

I know we struggle against evil on a heavenly plane as
much as on an earthly one (Eph. 6:12). Help me to teach my
child how to put on Your armor as soon as she is old enough,
Father, so that when evil looks her in the eye, at whatever age
it visits her, she can hold her ground with confidence
(Eph. 6:13).

In the meantime, I will partner with You by praying for this precious child of mine on all occasions and with all kinds of requests, and I will stay alert to the influences that surround her (Eph. 6:18). And even after she is old enough to pray on her own, I'll continue to pray as Jesus did: Please keep this child from temptation and deliver her from evil (Matt. 6:13).

You are our deliverer, Lord (Ps. 37:39-40). And today I thank You for every piece of Your priceless armor—and especially for being willing to remove it on the day You defeated Satan by dying for the sins of the world! Because You made Yourself vulnerable, now Baby and I don't have to be. Thank You!

In Your saving name I pray. Amen.

Sweet Tooth

How sweet are your words to my taste,
sweeter than honey to my mouth!

PRAYING PSALM 119

Lord, grant my baby a sweet tooth for Your words! How I long for him to grow up hearing the Bible spoken, cherished, and obeyed.

Help me to do my part every day to shape his taste buds. I want to bind the Word on his forehead and write it on the doorframes of his house, like those Jewish moms of old (Deut. 6:8-9). Nothing less will do.

Your Word can keep him from straying (v. 11).

Your Word can make him rich in ways that matter most (v. 4).

Your Word can bring him insight and delight (v. 24).

Your Word will strengthen him in weakness (v. 25) and comfort him in sorrow (vv. 28,50).

Your Word will reveal to him Your love (v. 41).

Your Word will set him free to really live (v. 45).

Open my child's eyes by Your Spirit to see wonderful things in Your Word (v. 105). May his familiarity with the Holy Scriptures from infancy make him "wise for salvation through faith in Christ Jesus" (2 Tim. 3:15).

Thank You, Father, that in keeping Your words there is great reward (Ps. 19:11). Today, I claim that reward again for my child.

In Jesus' name. Amen.

Family Tree

*We will tell the next generation the praiseworthy deeds of the
LORD, his power, and the wonders he has done.*

PSALM 78:4

Heavenly Father,
thank You that this baby is a gift to all
my descendants yet to be (Ruth 4:12-15). May
my baby be a source of joy and a testimony of Your
enduring love (Ps. 127:3). Thank You that _____ can be a
new green shoot on Your family tree. This miracle person
in my arms may someday grow up to have a baby, and
that baby have a baby…a gift to some happy father
and mother—and to the whole world—from
the loving God of life.
Let every
generation
praise You,
Lord (Ps. 145:4). Amen.

The Stuff of Prayers

This is the real challenge of our spiritual lives as parents:

to take our distracting thoughts,

not to mention the distracting nursing,

dressing, schoolwork, sibling fights, family vacations,

baths, stories, meetings, and bedtimes,

and make of them the prayers that are our lives.

NANCY FUCHS

Safe and Sound

He has saved me from death, my eyes from tears, my feet from
stumbling. I shall live! Yes, in his presence—here on earth!

PSALM 116:8-9, TLB

PRAYING PSALM 116

Wonderful Lord, would You believe that I'm already worried
about drugs, car wrecks, and bad friends? My baby can't even
speak yet, and I'm thinking about keeping her safe after she
gets her driver's license!

Today, Lord, I pray that You would remind me of Your
loving care that extends far into the future—after I'm even
more obviously not in control of my child's life.

Hear my prayer, Lord: I love You because You listen to me
when I cry out to You for mercy no matter how desperate,
repetitive, or scared I sound (vv. 1-4).

How many times You hear me praying when I fear for my

child's safety—in the car, in unsafe neighborhoods, late at night, with untrustworthy friends, in dangerous sports, on a bed of illness. Lord, You understand how troubled and anxious I can become for my baby. Death could so easily snatch her away (v. 3)!

But You've heard me wailing, "O Lord, preserve _____'s life" (v. 4)! You have always shown me Your kindness. You are full of compassion toward me and my baby (v. 5). You watch over Your little ones. When we are in great need, You rescue us (v. 6).

How can I repay You, Lord, for Your goodness to us (v. 12)? I will tell others about Your power to save (v. 13). I will keep the promises I've made to You (v. 14).

In Your precious name. Amen.

By Faith

Without faith it is impossible to please God.

HEBREWS 11:6

PRAYING HEBREWS 11

Gracious Lord, today my baby has complete faith in many things: that I will come when he cries, that he will be fed when he's hungry, and that everyone he sees will try to get him to smile.

But today I pray in advance, and in faith, that my baby will grow up to have great faith in You. May he learn how to be confident about what he expects and hopes for from You, even if he can't see any physical evidence of it happening (v. 1).

By faith, help him to understand that it was You who made the entire universe out of nothing (v. 3). And may all of his prayers be pleasing and acceptable to You because of his faith (v. 4). Like Enoch, may he grow up knowing that if he believes You exist and seeks You earnestly, You will reward him (vv. 5-6). By faith, let him be like Noah, who believed in impossible things like arks in the rain (v. 7). By faith, may he be like Abraham and follow You wherever You lead. May he always look forward in faith to the city whose architect and builder is God. Even if he can't see it. Especially if he can't (vv. 8-10).

By faith, may my baby grow up to be like the ancients of the Bible, choosing to follow You to the point of suffering and disgrace rather than chasing the easier way of the world (vv. 20-38). You say the righteous will live by faith, and it is by faith that I come before You. I humbly ask that You'll turn my baby's weaknesses into strengths (v. 34) and that one day You'll welcome him into Your kingdom and commend him for his faith (v. 39).

In Your Son's name. Amen.

Someday a Spouse

The LORD God said, "It is not good for the man to be alone.
I will make a helper suitable for him."

GENESIS 2:18

Holy Lord, how good it is to know that You have made (or will yet make) a mate suitable for my baby. I know it seems premature to be thinking about Baby getting married, but somewhere out there his/her future spouse may be taking a first step, speaking a first word. And I already want to pray!

For my baby's future mate, I pray for strong character, forged through perseverance (Rom. 5:4). May he/she grow to be a person of integrity, filled with and led by the Spirit (Eph. 5:18, Gal. 5:18). May he/she be patient, kind, good, faithful, gentle, and full of self-control (Gal. 5:22-23). And may my child develop those traits too.

Even now, I pray that both my baby and his/her future

spouse will protect their sexual purity (1 Tim. 5:22, Eph. 5:3). Give them a desire to save themselves only for each other. May each make a full and total commitment to You at a young age. And may theirs be a marriage blessed by both love and commitment (Eph. 5:2, Heb. 13:4). And, yes...by more babies!

Amen.

No Worries

Therefore do not worry about tomorrow.

MATTHEW 6:34

PRAYING MATTHEW 6:25-34

Blessed Savior, as I watch my baby try to eat her toes, I rejoice in her total lack of concerns. But I know that as she grows, cares will come. Hardships and fears will come. And someday, she'll be like me—having to work a lot at not worrying. (See, Lord? I'm worried about her being a worrier!)

You told us repeatedly not to worry because You knew that we would struggle with this. And so today this is my prayer (may it reach out to bless my child someday):

May my baby grow up to understand that her soul is more important than food and her body more important than clothes (v. 25). Show her the birds that fly overhead, Father. Say to her heart, "See how they don't need to sow or reap or store away in barns? That's because I feed them. And you, being more valuable than they, I will feed too" (v. 26).

Gently remind her, Lord, just as You do me, that worrying won't add a single hour to her life (v. 27) but that all her days are secure in Your hand. And when she frets about her wardrobe (as I still do—forgive me, Lord!), remind her that You will clothe her as gloriously as You clothe the lilies of the field (vv. 28-30).

Thank you, Father, that You already know exactly what my baby will need every day of her life (v. 32). And all she really needs to concern herself with is seeking Your kingdom and Your righteousness above her earthly needs (v. 33). Then You will take care of the rest.

All my baby's tomorrows I place in Your hands, for You've promised to take care of them (v. 34). And for that reason, I give You all of my tomorrows as well.

Amen.

Character Counts

> *The wisdom of the wise will perish,*
> *the intelligence of the intelligent will vanish.*
>
> ISAIAH 29:14

Father, my baby's not even walking and, as You know, I'm already bombarded with advice about his future: "A good preschool assures a good foundation." "Choose your child's college NOW." "Do you have flashcards for the highchair or learning tapes for the crib?"

Father, I'm surprised there isn't a Hooked on Phonics for the womb! Everything counts, or so I'm told.

But what counts with You is my baby's character. You're not concerned with how early he can count to ten but how much his whole life will count for Your kingdom.

And so, Father, as my baby's character is developing, I pray that he will grow to love You with all his heart, soul, and mind (Matt. 22:37-40). And though it costs him everything in terms of self-discipline and sacrifices, I pray that he would pursue true wisdom and understanding (Prov. 4:7).

If my baby does happen to grow up to be strong and athletic, famous or rich, let him not boast in any of these (that goes for his dad and me too). Instead, as you told Jeremiah, "Let him who boasts boast about this: that he understands and knows me, that I am the LORD" (Jer. 9:24).

Yes, I want You to bless my baby with the smarts he needs to learn algebra and geometry (give him extra wisdom there—and some for me too!). But most of all, Father, I pray that someday my child will grow up to declare with David, "I know that You are pleased with me.... In my integrity you uphold me and set me in your presence forever" (Ps. 41:11-12).

By Your grace I pray. Amen.

Holy Giggles

Sarah said, "God has brought me laughter."

GENESIS 21:6

Lord of laughter, how I praise You and thank You for my baby's laughter. Like Sarah, You have brought me laughter through this tiny babe. Today this is my prayer: May my baby know much laughter as well.

As she grows, give my child reason to laugh. Let her know that Your joy is her strength (Neh. 8:10). Cause her to revel in Your mercies, which are new every morning (Lam. 3:23). Speak to her heart words of comfort and grace. May she laugh with praise and thanksgiving from a heart that overflows.

And when she cries, remind her that it's You, Lord, who turns mourning into gladness (Jer. 31:13). And it's You who will wipe every last tear from her cheek one day (Rev. 7:17).

Grant my baby a merry heart which does good like

medicine (Prov. 17:22) and a hearty laugh that's evidence of a solid and steadfast faith. May it be said of her, "She can laugh at the days to come" (Prov. 31:25). May she delight herself always in You (Ps. 37:4) and find fullness of joy forever in Your presence (Ps. 16:11).

Thank You, Lord! Just as you brought Sarah and Abraham a bundle of laughter, You've brought one to our family too. It is with joy that I pray to You today.

Amen.

"I Am Always with You"

How precious to me are your thoughts, O God!
How vast is the sum of them!

PSALM 139:17

A LETTER TO BABY FROM GOD,
BASED ON PSALM 139

Dear Sweet Baby, I know you and love you! I created you in your mother's womb. I saw your tiny body growing from un-formed mystery to breathing miracle! And I want to tell you—you turned out perfectly (vv. 13-15)!

As you grow up, I will always be with you. There's nowhere on this earth where you could possibly get lost from Me. In darkness or in light, I'm there. When you go to sleep, when you wake up, I'm here—to comfort, guide, and protect you (vv. 7-12).

As I look into your beautiful face, I understand every expression, every fleeting feeling or wonderment. I know you, and I love you (v. 4)!

You are always on My mind, dear child! I have more thoughts about you than the ocean has grains of sand. Every day of your life is already written down in My book and has been since the beginning of time (vv. 16-17).

My deep desire is to lead you in the ways of eternal life so that one day you can live forever in heaven with Me. I love you that much (v. 24)!

Your Heavenly Father

Topical Index